Robert Burns the Democrat

Robert Burns the Democrat

J. R. Campbell

Douglas McLean Publishing

Published in Great Britain by

DOUGLAS McLEAN PUBLISHING
Coleford
Gloucestershire

Robert Burns the Democrat by J. R. Campbell
First published as Burns the Democrat 1945
Reprinted as Robert Burns the Democrat 1959

This new edition published 2009

British Library Cataloguing in Publication Data
A catalogue record for this book is available from the British Library

ISBN 978-0-946252-71-8

Typeset in Garamond

Printed in Great Britain

Contents

Foreword - About John Ross Campbell 6
The Social Background 11
Burns on the Social System 19
Burns and the Poor 23
Burns and Religious Reform 25
The Poet and Calvinism 28
The Poet Flays Hypocrisy 34
The Poet's Personal Religion 37
Burns, the Patriot 42
Burns in the Fight for Political Reform 46
Burns and the French Revolution 49
Burns and the Witch Hunt 53
The Dumfries Volunteers 68
A Rebel until Death 72

Foreword

About John Ross Campbell

John Ross Campbell was born the son of a slater-journeyman in Paisley, Scotland, in 1894. In his boyhood he was a brilliant scholar, but like many of his social class in those days, family economic circumstances meant Academe was denied him.

So, at fourteen, he left school to work as a grocer's assistant. Politically aware, at seventeen he joined the Social Democratic Federation and then the British Socialist Party. From those early days he was champion to the cause of the then much oppressed working class. He proved a gifted orator attracting large crowds wherever he spoke.

He was twenty when the Great War started. As a member of the Royal Naval Volunteer Reserve (RNVR). he was called to the Clydeside division of First Lord of the Admiralty Winston Churchill's 'Royal Naval Division' (RND). There was a surplus of Naval reservists, many thousands more than required for the fully crewed war-ships. So at the outbreak of war Churchill utilised this surplus by handing them khaki uniforms and rifles and after a short training they were to fight as infantrymen along side the Army.

Campbell's war record is astonishing. He fought in and miraculously survived the front-line horrors of several bloody battles. He was one of the pitifully few survivors of the decimated Benbow RND battalion at Gallipoli and he was on the Somme, where he was awarded the Military Medal for conspicuous bravery. Eventually and surely inevitably, he was disabled and honourably discharged in June 1918, shortly before the end of the war. He came away with a collection of entry and exit bullet wounds from an assortment of battles and as a result of frostbite from the dreadful trenches of the Somme, amputated feet.

In 1921 he married Sarah Carlin, also from Paisley. She was a war widow with five children, four boys and a girl. With her, he parented these, then two girls of his own and at 48, became guardian to his infant grandson.

After his return from the trenches Johnny Campbell, continued fighting; but now for the working class. In 1920, together with William Gallagher and Harry Pollitt, he was a founder member of the Communist Party, a member of its executive committee in 1923 and of its political committee in 1924.

He played a leading part in the Clyde Workers Committee movement and became editor of its newspaper '*The Workers' Weekly*'. It was that newspaper's infamous article—which, contrary to popular belief, was not written by him, but by Harry Pollitt—that appealed to the troops not to shoot at the workers during the impending General Strike, which prompted his arrest for sedition. An enormous public outcry was immediate and most people politically left-of-centre championed Campbell. George Bernard Shaw stood his bail. 'No! I am *not* worth one hundred pounds' retorted Shaw to the Justices enquiry as to his financial status, 'However, I *have* one hundred pounds.'

The Attorney General, Sir Patrick Hastings, realising Campbell's popularity and not least his impressive war record, concluded that any prosecution was likely to fail. With the encouragement of Ramsey MacDonald's Labour Cabinet and MacDonald's own conviction that 'the prosecution was ill-advised from the beginning', Sir Patrick decided to use his powers to drop the 'Campbell Case'. This was a serious constitutional mistake. It also was a bungle almost as ridiculous as the original arrest. Meanwhile, the Communists were overjoyed and claimed a victory for the workers. The first Labour Government admitted mishandling the case. More seriously, they confessed to interfering with the course of justice. The Conservatives quickly put down a motion of censure, but finally voted with the Liberals for a complete investigation. The Government could not accept this and so in 1924, after only nine months in power, they dissolved Parliament.

The following year, when the Conservatives had regained power, Johnny Campbell, who had moved his family and newspaper — now the *Sunday Worker* — to London, was again arrested together with William Gallagher, Harry Pollitt and nine other leading communists for dissemination of 'seditious' communist literature.' Five of the twelve were given one-year prison sentences. The others, including Campbell who had like Gallagher and Pollitt conducted his own defence, were told by the Old Bailey judge: *Those of you who will promise me that you will have nothing to do with this* [Communist] *association or the doctrines which it preaches; I will bind over to be of good behaviour in the future. Those who do not promise, I will send to prison.* Each of the seven answered 'No I will not' and each was sentenced to six months. Campbell spent his time in prison mastering the German language and later went on to become fluent in French and in Russian.

In 1930 the *Sunday Worker* became the *Daily Worker* with William Rust as editor. Campbell remained on the staff as assistant editor in special charge of industrial and economic affairs and was also very influential and active in Communist Party politics. He contested five Parliamentary elections including, in 1951, Woodford against Winston Churchill.

In 1954 he became editor of the *Daily Worker* until his retirement ten years later. After this he remained popular as a public speaker and lecturer. His knowledge of the British Trade Union and Labour movement was profound and his reputation for penetrating analysis and polemical brilliance made him much in demand.

Harry Pollitt wrote of Johnny Campbell:

> His clarity of thought and facile pen have done immeasurable service to the movement and he can deal devastating blows at the enemies of progress inside as well as outside the workers' ranks. A fluent pawky speaker he is equally at home explaining every detail of the Party's Trade Union or Wages policy, or with a wealth of quotations revealing the greatness of Scotland's poet, Robert Burns.'

In these last years his war-wounds again began to trouble him and finally in 1969, his 75th year, led to a fatal heart attack.

* * *

Johnny Campbell, a lifelong Burns' devotee and recognised authority on the Poet, first published *Robert Burns the Democrat* in 1945 with a further Burns' bicentenary edition in 1959. It is a skilful study, which in his clear and concise style leads the reader knowledgeably and gently through the social, political and economic circumstances relating to Burns' life and character.

Brendan Behan (1923–64), the Irish poet, playwright and novelist, upon finishing *Robert Burns the Democrat,* decided to send a verse message of congratulations to Johnny Campbell, which appeared in the 'Workers' Notebook' column of *The Daily Worker*:

Guid comrades of the Scots Committee
A brither Gael fra' Dublin City
Wad praise your pamphlet neat and pretty
On Robert Burns,
When broadcast cant frae puir auld Ayr
The stomach turns.
A gentleman did prove sae nice

That Robbie never mentioned lice
In ladies' heads,
Nor gentry's vice nor mourned the poor.
Nor yawned when Louis lost his head
With grief, ate neither cake nor bread,
For the royal whoor.

But, Johnny Campbell, your wee book
Has rescued Robbie frae the hook
Of those who Burns's memory took
Tae prove him dead.
Burns fights yet for liberty,
Be hangit to the BBC,
And, Johnny Campbell, thanks frae me,
Ye guid auld Red.

Robert Burns the Democrat was an important book in its time and remains relevant. It is essential and pleasurable reading to all interested in Burnsian literature and wishing to understand more of the man behind the name of Robert Burns.

Douglas McLean *

The friend of man the friend of truth,
    The friend of age and guide of youth,
Few hearts like his with virtue warm'd
    Few heads with knowledge so informed:
If there's another world, he lives in bliss;
    If there is none, he made the best of this.

(Robert Burns)

---

* Douglas McLean, publisher of this book, is proud that he is Johnny Campbell's grandson.

The Social Background

Robert Burns, Scotland's national poet, whose bicentenary will be celebrated in many lands this year [1959], was born on 25th January 1759 at a period of great social and political change in the Western world.

He was born thirteen years and three months after the clans, under Bonnie Prince Charlie, went down to defeat at Culloden. The opening shots in the American Revolution were fired when he was a lad of sixteen, and the Bastille was stormed when he was thirty years of age and had three years previously published the Kilmarnock editions of his poems. Thus he lived in a period of two great revolutions and was greatly influenced by them and by the development of the movement for political reform in his homeland.

His 'Ballad on the American War' showed that he was familiar with the military campaign in America and the consequent political repercussions in Britain.

When Burns was born, Scotland was just beginning to recover from the economic consequences of the union with England (1707). The union meant free trade with England and in the first half of the century the much more efficient industries over the Border had wrought havoc with the poorly-equipped Scots industries on the east side of the country. It was not until the trade of Glasgow with the American colonies, particularly the tobacco trade, began to develop on a large scale, that the long and painful struggle to improve Scotland's economy began to show substantial signs of progress.

The exploitation of the American colonies was a source of super-profits and of great capital accumulation in Glasgow, which was later to provide the means of stimulating economic development in the West of Scotland.

In Burns' boyhood, James Watt in Glasgow University was busily improving the steam engine, while his colleague, Adam Smith, the professor of moral philosophy was turning more and more from philosophy to political economy in his lectures. He was already entering the path which led to the publication of The Wealth of Nations, in which the policy of releasing emergent capitalism from the shackles of state regulations was powerfully expounded. This policy was to find its most ruthless application in Scotland in the not too distant future.

Linen manufacture in Burns' boyhood was still the predominant textile industry. It was carried on mainly in the homes of the workers, who were, however, falling into growing dependence on the merchants who supplied them with raw materials and took away the finished products to sell on the market. There was some factory development though it was yet slight. A similar set-up prevailed when linen began to be displaced by cotton in the latter part of Burns' lifetime.

The semi-independent weavers, earning a good living by eighteenth century standards when trade was booming, were a section of the people easy to organise and ever-ready to express their discontent. They were the backbone of the popular radical movements which began to sprout up towards the end of the century.

In Burns' time, therefore, factory capitalism was but slightly developed. Indeed the only mention of a large-scale capitalist enterprise in Burns is his quip on the new Carron Iron Works near Falkirk, founded in the year in which he was born.

Burns tried to see this industrial wonder, which was rather a white elephant in its early period, when visiting the neighbourhood on 26th September 1787, but the dour gateman refused to admit him.

His dourness in refusing admission was immortalised in :

> We cam na here to view your warks,
> In hopes to be mair wise
> But only, lest we gang tae Hell,
> It may be nae surprise,
> But when we tirl'd at your door,
> Your porter dought na beat us;
> Sae may, should we to Hell's yetts come,
> Your billy Satan sair us.

Still, maybe posterity may have lost a lot because Burns was deprived of a close-up view.

There was one aspect of the changing economy with which Burns was only too well acquainted—the sweeping changes which were then taking place in agriculture. The old strip system of farming, in which a peasant's holding was divided into a number of strips intermingled with those of his fellows, was passing away and in its place was coming in a compact consolidated farm, in which the owner of the land and the farmer, usually employing some hired labour, were interested in introducing the latest improvements. Unfortunately the rents were fixed at levels which proved to be ruinous if there was a poor harvest or a fall in prices.

> But Mousie, thou art no thy lane,
> In proving foresight may be vain:
> The best laid schemes o' mice and men
> Gang aft agley
> An lea'e us nought but grief and pain,
> For promised joy.

Burns' father and Burns were to know the heartbreaking worry of trying to make ends meet in a lean year.

Burns in 'The Cottar's Saturday Night' has left us a highly sentimentalised picture of the cottar — the small peasant who was being eliminated by the enclosures and by the advance of the new farming technique. It was the cottars' life, as Burns' upright, intensely religious father would perhaps have liked to see it; but the cardboard figures in the poem are far from resembling the real earth-bound cottars whose Saturday night was not always spent in reading the Bible and in singing psalms. The 'Holy Fair' and 'Hallowe'en' give a picture of Scots rural life, which is much more alive.

Burns himself was not a cottar but a tenant farmer—as was his father. For the farm at Mount Oliphant, his father paid an annual rent of £40 to £45. When following his father's death Burns and brother Gilbert rented the farm at Mossgiel they paid an annual rent of £90. Burns' Dumfries-shire venture, the Ellisland farm, was rented from Patrick Miller at a sum of £50 per annum for the first three years and thereafter £70 per annum, It must be said, however, that Burns' father entered on the vocation of a farmer with very little capital, and so had to stint his family in food and to grossly overwork them.

The hired ploughman in Burns' day received an annual wage of £7 per year plus food and lodgings. The £90 per year which Burns paid for Mossgiel was a comfortable lower middle class income in the Scotland of that period. Burns was therefore not a member of the dying peasantry. He was a member, though a poor and financially handicapped one, of the class of tenant farmers employing the new agricultural technique.

Burns felt himself to be a member of a class that was rising in the social scale and was claiming a wider share in the life of the country.

In Ayrshire, in the Edinburgh interludes and in Dumfries, Burns' bosom friends were of the rising middle class. In the circle of lawyers, doctors, schoolmasters and progressive clergymen, Burns moved on terms of complete intimacy.

So nothing could be more absurd than to represent Burns as a 'heaven-inspired peasant' born with a miraculous gift of poetry, emerging from a mass of country bumpkins to astonish the world. Burns' Ayrshire acquaintances, Gavin Hamilton and Robert Aiken, lawyers, John Goldie and Robert Muir, wine merchants, the Reverend John McMath and John Mackenzie, were men of high intelligence taking a deep interest in all of the questions of their time.

From 1730 onward Scotland was experiencing an intense intellectual development. Hume in philosophy and history, Adam Smith in moral philosophy and political economy, Principal Robertson in history, Alexander Monro in anatomy, are but a few of the famous names of the period. More important still was the fact that poetry in the Scots tongue was beginning to revive.

Allan Ramsay was to print some of the old Scots poems in the Evergreen collection and the Tea Table Miscellany. But such Scots poetic tradition as came to Burns was truncated. Dunbar, Henryson and the other great Scots poets of the 15th and 16th century, he did not have the opportunity of reading in full.

The most powerful and beneficial poetic influence on Burns was Robert Fergusson (1750-1774) whose mastery of the Scots tongue was second only to that of Burns himself. So Scotland's national poet grew up in a situation in some ways favourable to a further advance in Scots poetry. In relation to Scots songs Burns made himself the best-informed man of his day. He was in addition a keen student of all the religious, political and philosophical questions of his time. The man who wrote 'Holy Willie's Prayer' knew Calvinist theology inside-out, a fact that helped to give that powerful satire its lethal punch.

By the time he went to Edinburgh at the age of twenty-seven he was by any reasonable standard a well-educated man, a brilliant conversationalist (what a pity no one played Boswell to him) with an exceptionally retentive memory. The conception of Burns as a prickly, uncouth genius out of place in the Edinburgh salons is fantastic. On any discussions relating to poetry, philosophy, religion or politics, he could give points to most of those present.

Dugald Stewart, the philosopher and economist, who was six years older than Burns left an account which shows the impression he made on a keen and cultured mind. Writing of his first meeting with Burns, Stewart said:

> 'His manners were then, as they continued ever afterwards, simple, manly and independent; strongly expressive of conscious genius and worth; but with-out anything that indicated forwardness, arrogance or vanity. He took his share in conversation but not more than belonged to him... Nothing, perhaps, was more remarkable amongst his various attainments than the fluency and precision and originality of his language when he spoke in company; more particularly as he aimed at purity in his turn of expression and avoided more successfully than most Scotchmen the peculiarities of Scottish phraseology.'

Burns' education was, however, dearly bought. It was acquired after strenuous days of work on the farm. In youth and young manhood in his daily toil and in his studies Burns worked far beyond his physical capacities. The result was a strained heart, the source of recurring fits of melancholia, and one of the major causes (along with wholly incorrect medical treatment) which hastened his early death.

By the standards of the Scotland of his day he did not in adult life live in conditions of grinding poverty. But both as farmer and exciseman he had to work hard to earn every penny of his modest competence. He was oppressed, sometimes unduly, by the insecurity of his position. No doubt his work as a farmer and exciseman helped to keep his feet on the ground of reality, but he had neither that peace of mind nor freedom from economic worry that would have enabled him to concentrate on his literary work.

In the later years of his life he lived under the menace of political victimisation. He was undoubtedly frustrated by the fact that he could not publicly express, in all vigour, what he felt and thought on the major political struggle of his day. That he achieved so much under conditions of extreme nervous strain is the real miracle of Burns.

His achievements were vast. He was the forerunner of that brilliant galaxy of English romantic poets of the early 19th century and was acknowledged by them to be such.

In his work for Johnson's *The Scots Musical Museum* and for Thomson's *Select Scottish Airs* he rescued hundreds of the folk tunes (particularly the Highland tunes) of his country from impending oblivion and fitted with his immortal words; they remain a joy to all mankind.

His satires are amongst the most powerful ever written in exposure of humbug, hypocrisy and oppression. His epistles express in glorious rhythm, the joy of life and he made the life of the common man, his fears and hopes the theme of poetry in a way that remains unsurpassed.

What a pity that his countrymen in praising him, often indiscriminately, did not take to heart his injunction to encourage Scots literature.

> . . . if a' the land
> Would take the Muses' servants by the hand,
> Not only hear, but patronise, befriend them,
> And where ye justly can commend, commend them,
> And aiblins when they winna stand the test
> Wink hard and say. 'The folks hae done their best'
> Would a' the land do this, then I'll be caition,
> Ye'll soon hae Poets o' the Scottish nation
> Will gar Fame blow until her trumpet crack,
> And warsle Time and lay him on his back.

(*Scots Prologue for Mrs. Sutherland, 1790*).

Books have been written on the value of his contribution to poetry and song, but as our theme is 'Robert Burns, the Democrat,' we will, in this modest book, confine ourselves to Burns as the herald of the common people in their struggle for a higher and nobler way of life.

Burns on the Social System

The dominant section of the ruling class in Burns' day was the landlords. They controlled the sparse group of voters in the country and degraded even the House of Commons of that day with a Scottish representation that was beneath contempt.

Burns had always his eye on the reactionary section of this class and immortalised some of them in biting satire.

In 1786 he wrote the 'Address of Beelzebub' to the Earl of Breadalbane. The Earl and the Highland Society had met in Covent Garden, London,

> 'to concert ways and means to frustrate the design of 500 Highlanders, who, as the Society was informed by Mr. Mackenzie of Applecross, were so audacious as to attempt an escape from their lawful lords and masters whose property they are by emigrating from the lands of Mr...MacDonald of Glencary to the wilds of Canada in search of that fantastic thing—Liberty.'

The successful American Revolution was in everyone's mind, and Burns pictures the emigrating highlanders setting up institutions on the American model in their new surroundings.

Faith! you and Applecross were right
To keep the Highland hounds in sight:
I doubt na'! they wad bid nae better,
Than let them ance out owre the water,
Then up among thae lakes and seas,
They'll mak what rules and laws they please;
Some daring Hancock, or a Franklin
May set their Highland bluid a-ranklin';
Some Washington again may head them.
Or some Montgomerie, fearless, lead them;
Till (God knows what may be effected
When by such heads and hearts directed)
Poor dunghill sons of dirt an' mire
May to Patrician rights aspire!
Nae sage North now, nor sager Sackville,
To watch and premier o'er the pack vile,
And whare will you get Howes and Clintons
To bring them to a right repentance-
To cowe the rebel generation,
An' save the honour o' the nation?

THEY, an' be damned! what right hae they
To meat, or sleep, or light o' day?
Far less to riches, power, or freedom,
But what your lordship likes to gie them.

Beelzebub promises the Earl his due station in hell when he passes over.

Go on, my Lord! I lang to meet you,
An' in my. house at hame ' to greet you;
Wi' common lords ye shanna mingle,
The benmost neuk beside the ingle,

At my right han' assigned your seat,
'Tween Herod's hip an' Polycrate.

In the next generation the Highland lairds were driving their tenants away to make room for sheep.

The life of the more frivolous section of the landed gentryis scathingly depicted in 'The Twa Dogs.'

But gentlemen, an' ladies warst,
Wi' ev'n-down want o' wark are curst.
They loiter, lounging, lank an' lazy;
Tho' deil-haet ails them, yet uneasy;
Their days insipid, dull an' tasteless;
Their nights unquiet, lang an' restless.

An' ev'n their sports, their balls an' races,
Their galloping through public places,
There's sic parade, sic pomp an' art,
The joy can scarcely reach the heart.
The men cast out in party-matches,
Then sowther a' in deep debauches.
Ae night they're mad wi' drink and whoring,
Niest day their life is past enduring.

The ladies arm-in-arm in clusters
As great and gracious a' as sisters,
But hear their absent thoughts o' ither,
They're a' run deils an' jads thegither.
Whyles, owre the wee bit cup and plaitie,
They sip the scandal potion pretty;
Or lee lang nights wi' crabbit leuks
Pore owre the devil's picture books,
Stake on a chance a farmer's stackyard,
An' cheat like onie unhanged blackguard.

The factors who squeezed the last penny of rent from the unfortunate tenants were a very special target for Burns' anger.

> I've notic'd on our Laird's court-day,
> (An' monie a time my heart's been wae'},
> Poor tenant bodies, scant o' cash
> How they maun thole a factor's snash ;
> He'll stamp an' threaten, curse an' swear,
> He'll apprehend them, poind their gear;
> While they maun stan' wi' aspect humble
> An' hear it a' an' fear an' tremble.

In his autobiographical letter to Doctor John Moore, Burns explained that it was the factor of his father's first farm at Mount Oliphant who was depicted in this poem.

Above all Burns hated the pride and insolence of the reactionary gentry.

> While frosty winds blaw in the drift
> Ben to the chimla lug,
> I grudge a wee the great-folk's gift
> That live sae bien and snug.
>
> I tent less and want less
> Their roomy fire-side,
> But hanker and canker
> To see their cursed pride.
>
> (*Epistle to Davie.*)

Burns and the Poor

The deepest sympathy of Burns was reserved for the poor man especially:

> When they meet wi' sair disasters
> Like loss o' health, or want o' masters.

He thought there was no more pitiful spectacle in the whole of human existence than that of a man searching for work.

> See yonder poor, o'erlaboured wight,
> So abject, mean and vile,
> Who begs a brother of the earth
> To give him leave to toil,
> And see his lordly fellow worm,
> The poor petition spurn,
> Unmindful, tho' a weeping wife
> And helpless offspring mourn.

The neglected, poor man, in his old age, wrung his heart.

> Look not alone on youthful prime,
> Or manhood's active might
> Man then is useful to his kind
> Supported is his right.

But see him on the edge of life,
With cares and sorrows worn,
Then Age and Want—O' ill-matched pair!
Shew man was made to mourn.
(*Man Was Made to Mourn.*)

He was later to read and enjoy Thomas Paine's *Rights of Man* the first political work to advocate Old Age Pensions. But the poet was to be well over onr hundred years in his grave before the first niggardly old age pension scheme was inaugurated.

In none of the letters or poems of Burns are any drastic economic changes in the social system of his day envisaged.

He looked rather to the gradual economic progress of the tenant farmers, small manufacturers and the middle class in general to create the elements of a better order, with, of course, the more intelligent members of the working class admitted to their ranks. The political reforms which he supported were to contribute to this end by the removal of unjust privilege.

And so, in the 'Epistle to a Young Friend,' to Andrew Hunter Aiken, son of Robert Aiken to whom the 'Cottar's Saturday Night' was dedicated, the advice is given:

To catch Dame Fortune's golden smile
Assiduous wait upon her,
And gather gear by every wile
That's justify'd by honour,
Not for to hide it in a hedge,
Nor for a train-attendant,
But for the glorious privilege
Of being independent.

Burns and Religious Reform

No estimation of Scots history is of the slightest value that ignores the central role of the reformed churches.

The Church of Scotland in the 17th and early 18th centuries enjoyed a prestige unparalleled in any other Protestant land. It was the only institution in the country which gave the small man—the peasants, the artisans, the small traders and shopkeepers—a voice in the affairs of their country (for the Kirk did not stand outside politics) and when put to it they had defended it with their lives.

Burns was never blind to the progressive role which had been played by the Kirk in Scots history.

> The Solemn League and Covenant,
> Now brings a smile, now brings a tear,
> But sacred Freedom, too, was theirs ;
> If thou'rt a slave, indulge thy sneer.

But in Burns' day the Kirk was tending to degenerate into an odious spiritual and social tyranny. People were hauled before the spiritual Gestapo, the Kirk Session, for the most trivial offences. To be lax in attendance at Church, to be engaged in worldly pursuits on the Sabbath day—were quite considerable offences.

Sexual laxity in any form was a major offence and no modern state, with all its centralisation of power, would venture to tackle it in the dictatorial manner of the Kirk Session.

Even today the Scots Sabbath is an institution unique in Christendom. In Burns' day and for a long time afterwards it was the amazement of Europe.

In the early 19th century, the great Frenchman of letters, Stendhal, wrote:

> 'I shall say nothing of the terrible Scotch Sunday besides which London's is a positive jollification. This day, consecrated to the honour of heaven is the nearest approach to hell I have seen on earth. Said a Scotch-man to a French friend as they were returning from Church: 'Not quite so fast or people will think we are taking a walk.'

Sinners against the sexual moral code-and they were fairly plentiful in the rough, old rural Scotland-had to sit in a special seat in the Church—known as the 'Creepie Chair'—and be publicly reproved for their sins. If they were well-to-do people the Kirk Session would relax the rules. They might be permitted to endure the reproof while standing in their own pew.

It is such a situation which is depicted in the poem, 'The Rantin Dog, the Daddie o't,' said to have been given by Burns to Jean Armour when she was with child by him. In the poem it is the woman who is speaking. The Rantin Dog is, of course, the poet himself.

When I mount the creepie-chair
Wha will sit beside me there?
Gie me Rob, I'll seek nae mair
    The rantin dog, the daddie o't.

Wha will crack to me my lane?
Wha will mak me fidgin-fain?
Wha will kiss me o'er again?
    The rantin dog, the daddie o't.

The Poet and Calvinism

Orthodox Calvanism in the sixteenth, seventeenth and eighteenth centuries was a religion more concerned with fighting the Devil (who had practically acquired naturalisation in Scotland) than in worshipping God. 'To feel the smoke of Hell's fire in the throat...to stand beside a river of fire and brimstone broader than the earth and to think to be bound hand and foot and casten into the midst of it quick [i.e. alive] and then to have God locking the prison door, never to be opened for all Eternity.' So wrote Samuel Rutherford, one of Scotland's most famous divines. In the famous poem, 'The Holy Fair', where excellent poetry and high satire are combined, Burns describes a typical hell-fire sermon.

But now the Lord's ain trumpet touts
    Till a' the hills are rairin'
And echoes back return the shouts
    Black Russell is na spairin'
His piercin' words, like Highlan' swords
    Divide the joints an' marrow.
His talk of Hell, whare devils dwell,
    Our vera. sauls does harrow'
            Wi' fright that day.

A vast, unbottomed, boundless pit
    Fill'd fou o' lowin brunstane
Whase ragin' flame, an' scorching heat,
    Wad melt the hardest whun stane.
The half-asleep start up wi' fear,
    An' think they hear it roarin'
When presently it does appear
    'Twas but some neebor snorin'
            Asleep that day.

This grim Calvinism was being challenged in Scotland throughout the 18th century. From Francis Hutcheson, Professor of moral philosophy in Glasgow from 1729 to 1746 there stemmed many critical trends. The most extreme developed through David Hume to scepticism or, to use the more modern term, agnosticism. The main trend led to a cautious undermining of the old Calvinist dogmatism within the Church itself, a greater stress on morality and on the necessity of interpreting the dogmas of the Church in the light of current knowledge or 'common sense.' Some of the religious and moral conceptions found in the letters and poems of Burns are the purest Hutcheson.

By Burns' time, the controversy had reached an acute stage.

The struggle between the Auld Lichts, who defended orthodox Calvinism, and the New Lichts, who wanted some modification of the historic Calvinist doctrine, was shaking every parish.

Burns threw his weight against the Auld Lichts, 'the lads in black,' in favour of the New Lichts, the 'candid liberal band.'

Broadly speaking the Auld Lichts represented the popular masses—the small farmers and the artisans—while the New Lichts were representative of the middle classes in the towns and the progressive section of the country gentry .

A big issue in the struggle was the question of patronage.

The Auld Lichts, strong in popular support, were for the election of the ministers by the congregations. Some New Licht ministers owed their posts to patronage, the nomination of the minister by the patron, usually a local landlord.

In Burns' poem, 'The Ordination,' a struggle over the appointment of a Mr Mackinlay, an Auld Licht clergyman, is described. The patron, the Earl of Glencairn, had been responsible in teeth of considerable popular opposition, when he appointed a Mr Lindsay, a New Licht, as the first minister in charge of the Laigh Kirk, Kilmarnock, some time previously.

The appointment was said to be due to the influence of Mrs Lindsay, whose maiden name was Maggie Lauder. She had been housekeeper to the Earl.

When the time came to appoint a second-in-charge, the Earl had wisely taken account of popular feeling and appointed the Auld Licht—Mackinlay. It was an Auld Licht victory which Burns satirises in the verse:

> Curst common-sense, that imp o' hell
>   Cam in wi' Maggie Lauder.
> But Oliphant aft made her yell
>   An' Russell sair misca'd her:
> This day Mackinlay taks the flail
>   An' he's the boy will blaud her!
> He'll clap a shangan on her tail
>   An' set the bairns to daud her,
>   Wi' dirt this day.

In the 'Holy Fair' the poet satirises one of the massed communion services in which the congregation of a number of neighbouring parishes met together to hear a relay of sermons from the assembled clergymen.

Here some are thinkin' on their sins
An' some upo' their claes;
Ane curses feet that fyl'd his shins,
Anither sighs and prays.
On this hand sits a chosen swatch
Wi' screw'd-up, grace-proud faces,
On that a set o' chaps at watch,
Thrang winkin' on the lasses
To chairs that day.

How monie hearts this day converts
O' sinners and o' lasses.
Their hearts o' stane, gin night are gane
As saft as ony flesh is.
There's some are fou o' love divine
And some are fou o' brandy,
And monie jobs that day begin
May end in houghmagandie
Some ither day.

The most deadly attacks on the old theology-were to come. In his 'Address to the Deil' Burns goes after the terror of all Calvinist Scotland. His Satan is no arrogant Prince of Darkness, but a comic figure, almost a boozing crony, whom the bard slaps on the back and nudges in the ribs.

O Thou! whatever title suit thee
Auld Homie, Satan, Nick or Clootie
Wha in yon cavern grim an' sootie
Closed under hatches,
Spairges about the brunstane cootie,
To scaud poor wretches!

Hear me, auld 'Hangie,' for a wee,
And let poor damned bodies be;
I'm sure sma' pleasure it can gie,
Ev'n to a deil,
To skelp an' scaud poor dogs like me,
An' hear us squeal!

The 'Fall of Man' is sketched in Burns' own inimitable fashion.

Lang syne in Eden's bonnie yard,
When youthful lovers first were paired
And all the soul of love they shared,
The raptured hour,
Sweet on the fragrant flowery swaird
In shady bower.

Then you, ye auld, sneck-drawing dog!
Ye cam to Paradise incog,
An' play'd on man a cursed brogue,
(Black be your fa'!)
An' gied the infant warld a shog,
'Maist ruin'd a'.

One of the points in which Auld Licht and New Licht theologies were in conflict was whether if a sinner repented he would go to heaven. The Auld Lichts were adamant. Only if the sinner in question was pre-destined for heaven would his repentance matter. The New Lichts, applying 'curst commonsense,' thought the repented sinner was fairly safe. Burns went one better. He thought the devil himself should repent and so change the entire cosmic set-up.

But fare-you-weel, Auld. 'Nickie-Ben'!
O wad ye tak' a thought an' men'!
Ye aiblins might—I dinna ken—
Still hae a stake:
I'm wae to think upo' yon den,
Ev'n for your sake!

The Poet Flays Hypocrisy

The greatest blow he struck at religious bigotry was in opposition to the Kirk Session of Mauchline, which had charged his friend, Gavin Hamilton, with unorthodox behaviour, to wit:

1. Unnecessary absence from Church two Sabbaths in December and three Sabbaths in January together.

2. Setting out on a journey to Carrick on the third Sabbath of December.

3. Habitual, if not total, neglect of family worship

4. Abusive letter to the Session dated 13 March 1784.

Heading the spiritual Gestapo, who were pursuing Hamilton, was one William Fisher, a sound man of church discipline, but apt to skid morally.

Soon there began to pass from hand to hand in Ayrshtre Burns' most famous satire, 'Holy Willie's Prayer,' in which the elder is found instructing the Deity how to run the universe, not to speak of the village of Mauchline.

Oh Thou, that in the heavens does dwell
Wha, as it pleases best Thysel'
Sends ane to heaven an' ten to hell,
                A' for Thy glory
And no for onie guid or ill
                They've done before Thee

When frae my mither's womb I fell
Thou might hae plung'd me deep in hell,
To gnash my gooms and weep and wail
                In burning lakes
Where damned devils roar and yell
                Chained to their stakes.

Yet I am here, a chosen sample
To show Thy grace is great and ample
I'm here a pillar o' Thy temple
                Strong as a rock
A guide, a buckler, and example
                To a' Thy flock.

This is good Calvinist doctrine, stated without exaggeration and yet presented in such a way as to show its essential irrationality.

Willie has to admit his lurches from the path of virtue.

O Lord! yestreen, Thou kens, wi' Meg—
Thy pardon I sincerely beg
Oh may't ne'er be a living plague
To my dishonour
An' I'll ne'er lift a lawless leg
Again upon her.

Besides I further maun avow,
Wi' Leezie's lass three times, I trow—
But Lord, that Friday I was fou,
When I cam' near her;
Or else, Thou kens, Thy servant true
Wad never steer her.

In spite of all this, Willie, under the firm conviction that he is one of the chosen few, concludes his appeal—

But Lord, remember me and mine,
Wi' mercies temporal and divine,
That I for grace and gear may shine
Excelled by nane
And a' the glory shall be thine
Amen, Amen.

This was strong meat for the year 1784—and, indeed, the satire was not published in Burns' lifetime.

Enough has been said to show that Burns was no idle rhymer in an ivory tower, but a fighter giving two blows for one in the great controversies of the day.

The Poet's Personal Religion

Before discussing Burns' ultimate religious beliefs it is well to note his wide reading on the question. He sends an epistle to his 'auld comrade dear and brither sinner,' James Tennant of Glenconner.

> I've sent you here, by Johnie Simpson,
> Two sage philosophers to glimpse on:
> Smith, wi' his sympathetic feeling,
> An' Reid, to common sense appealing,
> Philosophers have fought and wrangled,
> An' meikle Greek an' Latin mangled,
> Till, wi' their logic-jargon tir'd,
> And in the depths of science mir'd,
> To common sense they now appeal—
> What wives and wabsters see and feel!
>
> (*To James Tennant of Glenconner.*)

The books mentioned are Adam Smith's *Theory of the Moral Sentiments* and Thomas Reid's *Enquiry into the Human Mind*—a none too successful reply to the sceptical philosophy of Hume. Admirers of Reid have said that he anticipated the famous German, Immanuel Kant's criticism of Hume. Admirers of Kant usually shudder at the very idea. That such difficult philosophical works should be exchanged between farmers, however, shows something of the intellectual quality of the times.

Burns urges his good friend to return the volumes quickly for he has little left to read except the more orthodox works of Bunyan, Brown and Boston.

Sae shortly ye shall see me bright
A burning an' a shining light.

There can be no reasonable doubt that Burns knew most of the literature-orthodox and unorthodox of his time and formed his own opinions.

People went astray from the paths of virtue because some were endowed with stronger passions than others.

Thou know'st that Thou hast formed me,
With passions wild and strong
And list'ning to their witching voice
Had often led me wrong.

(A Prayer in the Prospect of Death.)

I saw thy pulse's maddening play
Wild-send thee Pleasures' devious way,
Misled by Fancy's meteor-ray,
By passion driven;
But yet the light that led astray
Was light from Heaven.

(The Vision.)

All mankind were beset by the same passions, and liable, given the circumstances, to make the same mistakes. So let us be charitable.

Then gently scan your brother man,
Still gentler sister woman;
Tho' they may gang a kennin wrang,
To step aside is human.
One point must still be greatly dark,
The moving WHY they do it;
And just as lamely can ye mark,
How far perhaps they rue it.
Who made the heart, 'tis He alone
Decidedly can try us:
He knows each chord, its various tone,
Each spring, its various bias.
Then at the balance let's be mute.
We never can adjust it;
What's done we partly may compute,
But know not what's resisted.

(Address to the Unco Guid.)

A life beyond the grave he hoped for, but often doubted. His most frequent attitude to this question is contained in a letter which he sent to his dying friend, Robert Muir, a wine merchant of Kilmarnock.

'I trust the spring will renew your shattered frame and make your friends happy. You and I have often agreed that life is no great blessing on the whole. The close of life, indeed to the reasoning eye is—

Dark as was chaos, ere the infant sun
Was rolled together or had tried his beams
Athwart the gloom profound.

But an honest man has nothing to fear. If we lie down in the grave, the whole man a piecc of broken machinery, to moulder with the clods of the valley-be it so; at least there is an end of pain, care, woes and wants.

If that part of the mind does survive the apparent destruction of the man--away with old wives' preju-dices and tales. Every age and every nation has a different set of stories; and as many are always weak of consequence they have often, perhaps always, been deceived.

A man conscious of having acted an honest part among his fellow creatures; even granting that he may be the sport, at times, of passions and instincts, he goes to a great Unknown Being who could have no other end in giving him existence but to make him happy, who gave him those passions and instincts and well knows their force.

These my worthy friend are my ideas, and I know that they are not far different from yours. It becomes a man of sense to think for himself; particularly in a case where all men are equally interested and where, indeed, all men are equally in the dark.'

(Letter to Robert Muir, 7th March 1788.)

On one thing Burns never wavered—the existence of a good, benevolent God. This he deduced from philosophy—from the assumed character of the human mind.

'Still there are two great pillars that bear us up amid the wreck of misfortune and misery. The one is composed of the different modifications of a certain, stubborn something in man, known by the name of courage, fortitude, magnanimity. The other is made up of those feelings and sentiments which, however the sceptic may deny them, or the enthusiast disfigure them, are yet, I am convinced, original and component parts of the human soul; those senses of the mind, if I may be allowed the expression, which connect us with, and link us to those awful obscure realities—an all powerful and equally beneficent God, and a world to come, beyond death and the grave. The first gives us the nerve of combat while a ray of hope beams in the field; the last pours the balm of comfort into the wound which time can never cure.'

(Letter to A[exander Cunn;ngham, 25th February 1794.)

Despising the Holy Willies, Burns did not pray for 'grace and gear,' but for wit and sense.

O Thou wha gies us each good gift,
Gie me o' wit and sense a lift,
Then turn me, if Thou please, adrift,
  Thro' Scotland wide,
Wi' cits nor lairds I widna shift,
In a' their pride.

Were this the charter of our state
'On pain o' hell be rich and great'
Damnation then would be our fate
    Beyond remead;
But, thanks to heaven, that's no the gate
    We learn our creed.

For thus the royal mandate ran,
When first the human race began,
'The social, friendly, honest man,
        Whatever he be,
'Tis he fulfils great Nature's plan,
        And none but he.'

(2nd Epistle to Lapraik.)

Burns worshipped a God of love and human brotherhood.

But deep this truth impress'd my mind,
  Thro' all His works abroad,
The heart benevolent and kind,
  The most resembles God.

(A Winter Night.)

Burns, the Patriot

Burns grew to manhood in a period when the flame of Scots nationality was weak and fitful. The Act of Union, which subordinated Scotland politically and industrially to England, was regarded as an irreversible fact, likely to lead to the elimination of all those characteristics which distinguished the Scots from the English. The forces which impeded this prospect of complete Anglicisation and which will yet grow strong enough to win for the Scots their own Parliament, with complete right of self-determination once again, grew but slowly. Burns' poetry was, however, a powerful obstacle to any further deterioration of the national spirit.

In his famous autobiographical letter to Dr. John Moore (father of the general who died at Corunna in the Peninsular War) Burns says 'the first two books I ever read in private, and which gave me more pleasure than any two books I ever read again, were the life of Hannibal and the history of Sir William Wallace. Hannibal gave my young ideas such a turn that I used to strut in raptures up and down after the recruiting drum and bagpipe, and wish myself tall enough to be a soldier; while the story of Wallace poured a Scottish prejudice in my veins, which will boil along there till the floodgates of life shut in eternal rest.'

The Wallace theme constantly recurs in his poetry.

We'll sing auld Coila's plains an' fells,
Her moors red-brown wi' heather bells,
Her banks and braes, her dens and dells,
        Whare glorious Wallace
Aft bure the gree, as story tells,
        Frae Suthron billies.

At Wallace' name, what Scottish blood
But boils up in a spring-tide flood,
Oft have our fearless fathers strode
        By Wallace' side
Still pressing onward, red-wat-shod,
        Or glorious died.

(To William Simpson of Ochiltree.)

In his Scots prologue which Mrs. Sutherland recited on her benefit night in the theatre at Dumfries in 1790, he asked Scots poets to turn to their own history for themes.

Is there no daring Bard will rise and tell,
How glorious Wallace stood, how hapless fell?
Where are the muses fled that could produce,
A drama worthy o' the name o' Bruce?
How here, even here, he first unsheathed the sword
Gainst mighty England and her guilty lord,
And after monie a bloody deathless doing,
Wrenched his dear country from the jaws of Ruin!

Sometimes Burns' nationalism took the form of a sentimental look backwards at the Jacobite past.

But why of that epocha make such a fuss
That gave us the Hanover stem,
If bringing them over was lucky for us,
I'm sure 'twas as lucky for them.

But loyalty—truce! we're on dangerous ground:
Who knows how the fashions may alter?
The doctrine, to-day that is loyalty sound,
To-morrow may bring us a halter.

(To William Tytler.)

Or the better known lines written on a window at Stirling:

The injured Stuart line is gone,
A race outlandish fills their throne;
An idiot race, to honour lost,
Who know them best despise them most.

The most powerful attack on the Act of Union is in volume IV of the Scots Musical Museum, published in June 1792.

Fareweel to a' our Scottish fame,
Fareweel our ancient glory,
Fareweel even to the Scottish name
Sae famed in martial story.
Now Sark rins over Solway sands,
An' Tweed rins to the ocean,
To mark where England's province stands
Such a parcel of rogues in a nation.

What force or guile could not subdue,
Thro' many warlike ages,
Is wrought now by a coward few
For hireling traitors' wages.
The English steel we could disdain,
Secure in valour's station,
But English gold has been our bane—
Such a parcel of rogues in a nation.

O, would, or I had seen the day
That Treason thus could sell us,
My auld grey head had lien in clay
Wi' Bruce and loyal Wallace,
But pith and power, till my last hour,
I'll make this declaration—
We're bought and sold for English gold,
Such a parcel of rogues in a nation.

What with Marshall aid, military aid and other American bribes to reduce the independence of the whole island and to install nuclear bases in it, this poem is surely as apposite as ever:

Now, for my friends' and brethren's sakes
And for my dear-loved Land o' Cakes
I pray with holy fire—
Lord, send a rough-shod troop o' hell,
O'er a' wad Scotland buy or sell,
To grind them in the mire!
(Election Ballad addressed to Graham of Fintry, 1790.)

And in the bicentenary year of the poet [1959], so say all of us.

Burns in the Fight for Political Reform

The Scots in Burns' time were a politically defranchised people. Only 3,000 people in the country had votes and every one of these voters had a price—money, a government appointment or some other inducement to ensure that they cast their votes in defence of privilege.
Burns referred to this in his poem on 'The Fete Champetre' (The Garden Party).

> Come, will ye court a noble lord,
> Or buy a score o' lairds, man,
> For Worth and Honour, pawn their word,
> Their vote shall be Glencaird's, man.
> Ane gies them coin, ane gies them wine,
> Anither gies them clatter,
> Annbank, wha guess'd the ladies' taste
> He gies a Fete Champetre.

Virtually all the votes were controlled by a handful of rich merchants, or landed gentry, who in turn were controlled by the King's representative in Scotland—Henry Dundas. The Scottish vote could be generally relied on to support any measures for undermining the liberty of the United Kingdom, in general, or Scotland in particular.

What Burns thought of some of those chosen by the King—the half-mad George III—will be found in the poem called 'A Dream,' which is prefaced by the lines:

> Thoughts, words and deeds, the Statute
> Blames with reason,
> But surely DREAMS were ne'er indicted treason.

Addressing the King Burns says:

> Far be't frae me that I aspire
> To blame your legislation,
> Or say ye wisdom want, or fire to rule
> To rule this mighty nation,
> But faith! I muckle doubt, my Sire
> Ye've trusted ministration
> To chaps wha in a barn or byre,
> Wad better fill'd their station,
> Than courts yon day.

Under the guise of loyalty, Burns slipped in a few neat criticisms of the royal princes, who, truth to tell, were amongst the most useless rakes in all the royal families of Europe.

> For you young Potentate o' Wales,
> I tell your Highness fairly,
> Down Pleasure's stream wi' swelling sails,
> I'm tauld ye're driving rarely,
> But some day ye may gnaw your nails,
> An' curse your folly sairly
> That ye ever brak Diana's pales,
> Or rattled dice wi' Charlie,
> By night or day.

The Royal Princesses are urged to 'marry British.'

Ye, lastly, bonie blossoms a'
Ye royal lassies dainty,
Heaven mak ye guid as well as braw
An' gi'e ye lads a-plenty,
But sneer na British boys awa'
For kings are unco' scant ay
An' German gentles are but sma'
They're better just than want ay
On onie day.

As a good democrat Burns never lost an opportunity of emphasising the common humanity of people belonging to the most diverse ranks of society.

He addressed the louse, creeping up a fine lady's bonnet:

Ye ugly, creeping, blastit wonner,
Detested, shunned by saunt an' sinner,
How daur ye set your tit upon her,
Sae fine a lady.
Gae somewhere else and seek your dinner,
On some poor body.

O Jenny, dinna toss your head,
An' set your beauties a' abread,
Ye little ken what cursed speed
The blastie's makin';
Thae winks and finger-ends I dread,
Are notice takin'

O wad some Power the giftie gi'e us
To see oursels as ithers see us,
It wad frae monie a blunder free us
An' foolish notion:
What airs in dress an' gait wad lea'e us,
An' ev'n devotion.

(To a Louse.)

Burns and the French Revolution

When the great French Revolution broke out in 1789, it fanned the flames of political reform in Scotland. All over the country reforming societies were formed demanding an extension of the franchise and shorter parliaments. Burns was a strong supporter of political reform and was roused to enthusiasm by the French Revolution. In the beginning of 1792, when he was settled in Dumfries, he was one of a mixed party of dragoons and excisemen who captured a smuggler's brig, *The Rosamond.* The armament of the brig was put up for auction and Burns bought four small cannon which he sent as a gift to the French National Assembly. There was, of course, nothing illegal in this act. Britain was not at that moment at war with France. Nevertheless the government of the day utterly detested the democratic principles of the French Revolution, and Burns' act was doubtless noted by the authorities.

Supporters of political reform, when they met for a convivial evening, were fond of expressing their sentiments in seditious toasts.

One of Burns' favourite toasts was:

> 'To the last verse, of the last chapter, of the last Book of Kings.'

When the Edinburgh Gazetteer was founded, to champion the cause of political reform, Burns wrote to the editor, William Johnstone:

> 'Go on, Sir! Lay bare with undaunted heart and steady and the horrid mass of corruption called politics and statecraft. Dare to draw in their native colours these 'calm thinking villians, whom no faith can fix,' whatever the Shibboleth of their pretended party.'

At the very moment when the Government was preparing to curtail the very limited rights of free speech then existing, Burns sends to the *Gazetteer* the poem, 'Here's a Health to Them That's Awa'.'

> May Liberty meet wi' succcess
> May Prudence protect her frae evil,
> May tyrants and tyranny tine i' the mist,
> And wander their way to the devil!
>
> Here's freedom to them that wad read,
> Here's freedom to them that wad write,
> There's nane ever fear'd that the truth should be heard,
> But they whom the truth would indite.

In July 1792 the Society of the Friends of the People was formed in Edinburgh and made clear that it stood for reform on the basis of Kings, Lords and Commons in Parliament. One of its leaders was Lord Daer, whom Burns had met some years before at the house of Dugald Stewart.

Then from his Lordship I shall learn,
Henceforth to meet with unconcern,
One rank as well's another,
Nae honest, worthy man need care,
To meet with noble youthfu' Daer,
For he but meets a brother.

(Lines on Meeting Lord Daer.)

Branches of Friends of the People shot up all over Scotland embracing not only sections of the Whig gentry and the urban middle class, but also the artisans (particularly the weavers) and the small shopkeepers.

On 26th November 1792 Burns sent to Miss Louisa Fontenelle, the leading lady in a company playing in the theatre at Dumfries a prologue entitled 'The Rights of Women.' The background of the times is neatly sketched in the opening lines:

While Europe's eye is fix'd on mighty things,
The fate of empires and the fall of kings
While quacks of state must each produce his plan
And even children lisp the Rights of Man;
Amid this mighty fuss just let me mention,
The Rights of Women merit some attention.

After some high flown compliments to women the prologue concludes:

But truce with kings, and truce with constitutions,
With bloody armaments and revolutions;
Let Majesty your first intention summon,
Ah! Ça Ira! THE MAJESTY OF WOMAN.

A few days later he asks her to put on a play entitled 'The Wonder A Woman Keeps A Secret.' This was an undistinguished piece but it contained one or two platitudes

about British liberty, which could be given political point by well-timed applause. Such political demonstrations were common at a time when people had to be discreet in exercising free speech. It may have been during the performance of this play that Burns was involved in an incident which was duly reported to his superiors in the Government service. At the end of a performance some of the people in the best seats called for the orchestra to play 'God Save the King,' and were countered by a group in the pit who called for the French revolutionary anthem 'Ça Ira.' Amongst the group was the poet himself, though he denied taking part in the demonstration. But his general sentiments were known and
he was regarded by the local reactionaries as the leader. In a letter to Mrs. Dunlop he describes the incident as follows:

> 'We in this country here have many alarms of the Reform, or rather the Republican Spirit of your part of the Kingdom. Indeed we are in a good deal of commotion ourselves and in our theatre here 'God Save the King' has met with some groans and hisses, while 'Ça Ira ' has been repeatedly called for.
>
> For me, I am a placeman, you know, a very humble one indeed heaven knows, *but still so much so as to gag me from joining in the cry*. (Italics ours).
>
> What my private sentiments are you will find without an interpreter.
>
> In the meantime I have taken up the subject in another view and the other day for a pretty actress's benefit I wrote an address which I will give on the other page, called the "Rights of Woman".'

Burns and the Witch Hunt

At the beginning of December 1792 a convention of the Friends of the People Society met in Edinburgh to plan the campaign for reform. It again made it clear that its policy was reform and not revolution by repeating that it stood on the basis of King, Lords and Commons. A delegation from the United Irishmen attended and presented an address whose militant tone alarmed some of the delegates. So the address was read but was not formally received. The convention, however, ended its proceedings with the delegates standing with hands uplifted swearing to 'live free or die.'

Five days later on 13th December 1792 in London, Thomas Paine, the author of the '*Rights of Man,* 'was indicted (in his absence) of uttering a 'seditious libel.' The *Rights of Man* (with its defence of the principles of the French revolution and of republican principles in general) was the text book of the more militant reformers, and the Government believed that by designating it as a seditious libel it could suppress the book and arrest all who were trying to circulate it.

In his absence Paine was defended by the great Scots-born advocate, Thomas Erskine ('Here's a health to Tammie, the

Norland laddie, the lives at the lug of the law,' Burns had written in the *Edinburgh Gazetteer*, a reform paper). Erskine's speech was a masterpiece of legal argument, but the bribed jury found that the *Rights of Man* 'was a seditious libel' and Paine was outlawed. On the basis of this verdict the Government proceeded to arrest any reformers guilty of circulating the *Rights of Man*.

It was in this atmosphere that Burns learned that the Board of Excise had started an enquiry into his political opinions. He wrote to his patron, Robert Graham of Fintry, denying the allegations of political disaffection and pleading for his wife and children.

> 'Sir, you are a husband and a father, you know what you would feel to see the much loved wife of your bosom and your helpless prattling little ones turned adrift into the world, degraded and disgraced, from a situation in which they had been respectable and respected and left almost without the necessary support of a miserable existence.'

Burns, like many authors before him and since, had decided not to court victimisation, but to play for safety for the time being without, however, changing his opinions.

A few days after the letter to Graham of Fintry, he dispatches one of a different kind to Mrs. Dunlop, announcing that:

> '. . . some envious malicious devil has laid a little demur on my political principles and I wish to let the matter settle before I offer myself too much in the eyes of my superiors. . . I have set, henceforth, a seal on my lips as to those unlucky politics; but to you I must breathe my sentiments.'

Unfortunately, the portions of the letter in which Burns breathes his sentiments is missing, but they can be gathered from a letter a few days later which he sent to the same lady.

> 'For this instance, the amiable circle I so lately mixed with in the hospitable hall of Dunlop—their gentle, generous hearts; their uncontaminated, dignified minds; their informed and polished understandings—what a contrast when compared—if such comparings were not downright sacrilege—with the prostituted soul of the miscreant wretch who can deliberately and diabolically plot the destruction of an honest man who never offended him, and with a grin of satisfaction can see the unfortunate man, his faithful wife, and prattling innocents, turned over to Beggary and Ruin.'

On the same date he dispatched a letter to Graham of Fintry admitting he was in the pit of the theatre when the cry for 'Ça Ira' went up, and that—'one or two individuals with whom I occasional associate were of the party.'

But he denies either joining in the shout or of taking any part in the attempt to quell the subsequent free fight. He affirms his belief in the British Constitution but believes—

> '. . . that we have a good deal deviated from the original principles of that Constitution, particularly that an alarming system of Corruption has pervaded the connection between the Executive Power and the House of Commons.
>
> As for France, I was her enthusiastic votary at the beginning of the business. When she came to show her old avidity for conquest in annexing Savoy, etc., to her dominions, and invading Holland, I altered my sentiments!'

From Edinburgh Burns' friend, William Nicol, the classical master in the High School, wrote a letter counselling discretion.

> 'Dear Christless Bobbie,
> What is become of thee? Has the Devil flown off with thee as the Gled does with a bird? If he should do so there is little matter if the reports concerning thy imprudence are true. What concerns it thee whether the lousy Dumfriesian fiddlers play ' Ça Ira' or 'God Save the King? Suppose you had an aversion to the King, you could not as a gentleman wish God to use him worse than he has done.' (A reference to the madness of King George III.)

The danger to Burns had evidently blown over by 20th February 1793, when he replied to Nicol in a real rollicking vein:

> 'O thou wisest among the wise, meridian blaze of Prudence, full moon of Discretion and chief of many Counsellors.
>
> How infinitely is thy puddle-headed, rattle-headed, wrong-headed round-headed slave, indebted to thy super-eminent goodness, that from the luminous path of thy own right-handed rectitude, you lookest benignly down on an erring wretch of whom the zig-zag wanderings defy all the powers of Calculation, from the simple copulation of Units up to the hidden mysteries of fluxions.
>
> May one feeble ray of that light of wisdom which darts from thy sensorium, straight as the arrow of Heaven against the head of the Unrighteous, and bright as the meteor of inspiration descending on the holy and undefiled Priest-hood—may it be my portion, so that I may be less unworthy of the face and favour of that

> father of Proverbs and master of Maxims, that antipode of folly, and magnet among the sages, the wise and witty Willy Nicol. Amen, Amen, Yea, so be it.'

Among Burns' admirers who were willing to stand by him financially in the event of his victimisation was John Francis Erskine of Mar. In a letter dated 13th April 1793, the poet tells him that the trouble had blown over. It appears that Graham of Fintry had laid Burns' explanatory letter before the Board of Excise, and some of the Board (doubtless because the hat fitted) had taken exception to the remarks on political corruption, so—

> '. . . one of our supervisors general, a Mr. Corbett, was instructed to enquire, on the spot, into my conduct and to document me—' that my business was to act and not to think and whatever might be men or measures, it was for me to be silent and obedient.' Mr. Corbett was likewise my steady friend; so between Mr. Graham and him, I have been partly forgiven.'

It was after that experience that the poet penned the well known lines:

In politics if thou wouldst mix
And mean thy fortunes be,
Bear this in mind, be deaf and blind,
Let great folk hear and see.

While Burns was sidestepping the witch-hunters, the Scottish Reformers were being hounded. Thomas Muir, a young lawyer who was their outstanding leader, was arrested in January 1793, but was let out on bail. He went to France in the meantime in an attempt to dissuade the French Convention from imposing the death penalty on Louis XV. But he was too late.

He returned to Britain in July and stood trial in August, defending himself brilliantly. His chief offence was recommending the works of Paine and in insisting that the address of the United Irishmen should be read at the Convention the previous December. The notorious Lord Braxfield presided over the trial and told the jury that 'Mr. Muir might have known that no attention could be paid to such a rabble [of ignorant weavers]. What right had they to representation?'

The jury thus instructed returned a verdict of guilty and Muir was sentenced to fourteen years' transportation to Botany Bay.

On 12th September the Reverend Thomas Fyshe Palmer, a Unitarian minister in Dundee, was sentenced to seven years' transportation. He had revised a pamphlet explaining Paine's principles for the Dundee Friends of Liberty and had encouraged people to read the works of Paine.

Palmer's main crime in the eyes of the judge was that he had sought to organise mechanics 'and those whose circumstances and education do not entitle them or qualify them to judge of matters of legislation.' In a poem circulated a year later, 'From Esopus to Maria,' Burns characterises his attitude at this period.

> The shrinking Bard adown the alley skulks,
> And dreads a meeting worse than Woolwich hulks,
> Though there his heresies in Church and State
> Might well award him Muir and Palmer's fate.

Muir and Palmer were confined in Woolwich hulks prior to transportation to Botany Bay.

It was very difficult to keep Burns down for long. In spite of the mounting persecution he can still sing a song to 'Liberty and Independence.' So in August 1793, the month in which Thomas Muir was sentenced, he sent 'Scots Wha Hae' to Thomson in Edinburgh and describes how he came to write it—

> 'I shewed the air to Urbani who was highly pleased with it and begged me to make soft verses for it, but I had no idea of giving myself any trouble on the subject, till the accidental recollections of that glorious struggle for freedom, associated with the glowing ideas of some other struggles of the same nature, *not quite so ancient,* roused my rhyming mania.' (Italics ours.)

Not merely the defeat of the 'Auld Enemy'—England, but the French Revolution and 'Muir and Palmer's fate' was stirring Burns when he wrote:

> Lay the proud Usurpers low;
>   Tyrants fall in every foe,
> Liberty's in every blow
>   Let us do or die.

In short, the oath of the convention of the Society of Friends of the People to ' live free or die' in another form.

In spite of the mounting hysteria the Friends of the People called another convention which met in Edinburgh on 19th November 1793. There were forty-five Scottish societies present, four delegates from the English societies and three from the Society of United Irishmen. The official title of the convention was 'The British Convention of Delegates of the People Associated to obtain Universal Suffrage and Annual Parliaments.'

On the morning of 3rd December the convention's secretary, William Skirving, was arrested with other leading delegates, including Maurice Margarot and Joseph Gerrald of the London Correspondence Society. The Lord Provost of Edinburgh then dispersed the convention. Skirving and Gerrald, released on bail, gathered the delegates together for an evening session which was dispersed by the Sheriff-

Substitute and a further attempt to continue the convention at Skirving's house was forbidden by the magistrates.

Skirving, Margarot and Gerrald were tried separately by Braxfield and were each sentenced to fourteen years' transportation.

Gerrald at his trial protested against the word reformer being used as a term of abuse. After all, Jesus Christ was a reformer he said, whereupon Braxfield retorted, 'Muckle ye make o' that: he was hanget.'

In this period of suppression Burns may have written the 'Tree of Liberty' which some past editors of his works classified as doubtful. Henley rejected it on the grounds of its poetic worthlessness. With his estimation of its poetical values we agree, but the worthy Henley was doubtless annoyed by what he considered its political worthlessness. Here are some specimen verses:

Heard ye o' the tree o' France,
And wat ye what's the name o't?
Around it a' the patriots dance.
Weel Europe kens the fame o't.
It stands where ance the Bastille stood.
A prison built by kings, man.
Where superstition's hellish brood
Kept France in leading strings, man.

But vicious folk aye hate to see
The works o' Virtue thrive man,
The courtly vermin banned the tree
And grat to see it thrive, man.
King Louis thought to cut it down
When it was unco sma', man,
For this the watchman crack'd his crown,
Cut aff his head and a', man.

Wi' plenty o' sic trees I trow,

The warld would live in peace, man,
The sword would help to mak' a plough,
The din o' war wad cease, man,
Like brethren in a common cause,
We'd on each other smile, man,
And equal rights and equal laws,
Wad gladden every isle, man.

'Why Should We Idly Waste Our Prime' is another poem the cautious editors have classified as doubtful.

Why should we idly waste our prime,
Repeating our oppressions?
Come rouse to arms, 'tis now the time,
To punish past transgressions.
'Tis said that kings can do no wrong,
Their murderous deeds deny it.
And since from us their power is sprung,
We have a right to try it,
Now each true patriot's song shall be
'Welcome death or libertie.'

The golden age we'll then revive,
Each man will be a brother,
In harmony we all shall live,
And share the earth together.
In virtue trained, enlighten'd youth,
Will love each fellow creature,
And future years shall prove the truth
That man is good by nature.
Then let us toast with three times three
The reign of Peace and Libertie.

In the middle of 1794 Burns was present at a Saturday night

party in Dumfries where one of his seditious toasts got him into trouble with a certain Captain Dods. In fact the Captain abused Burns so fiercely that—

> '. . . had I had nobody's welfare to care for other than my own, we would certainly have come according to the manners of the world to the necessity of murdering one another about the business.
>
> The words [i.e., of Captain Dods—J.R.C.] were such as generally, I believe, end in a brace of pistols, but I am still pleased to think that 1 did not ruin the peace and welfare of a wife and a family of children in a drunken squabble.'

The toast which related to the war which Britain was then waging with revolutionary France, was:

> 'May our success in the present war be equal to the justice of our cause.'

This Burns argued in a letter he wrote the following morning, when he was a soberer and a wiser man, was:

> 'A toast that the most outrageous frenzy of loyalty cannot object to.'

The valiant Captain evidently thought otherwise. Maybe it was not what Burns said but the nasty way he said it that aroused his loyalist ire.

The Captain was not subject to any misunderstanding for about the same time Burns was writing to George Thomson, in Edinburgh:

> 'Is there no news yet, my dear Sir, of Pleyel. Or is your work to be at a dead stop until these glorious Crusaders,

the Allies, set our modern Orpheus at liberty from the savage thraldom of Democrat Discords.

Alas the day! And woe is me! That auspicious period, pregnant with the happiness of millions—that golden age, spotless with Monarchical innocence and Despotic purity—that Millennium of which the earliest dawn will enlighten even Republican turbulence and show the swinish multitude they are but beasts, and like beasts must be led by the nose and goaded in the backside—these days of sweet chords and concords seem by no means near.'

In short the success of the Allies in the war with revolutionary France was 'equal to the justice of their cause'—they were being heavily defeated. And so Burns lets himself go with a swing:

When princes and prelates and hot-headed zealots
All Europe had set in a lowe,
The poor man lies down, nor envies a crown,
But comforts himself with a mowe,

When Brunswick's great Prince cam a cruising to France,
Republican billies to cowe,
Bauld Brunswick's great Prince wad shown better sense,
At home wi' his Princess to mowe.

Out over the Rhine, proud Prussian wad shine,
To spend his best blood he did vow,
But Frederick had better, ne'er forded the water,
But shout as he docht in a mowe.

By sea and by shore the Emperor swore
In Paris he'd kick up a row,
But Paris sae ready just leugh at the laddie

And bade him gae tak him a mowe.

Meanwhile the Government was following up the suppression of the Convention in Edinburgh by prosecutions of reformers all over England. In May 1794 it arrested a number of leading London reformers, Thomas Hardy, John Home Tooke and James Thelwall, representing three reform societies. By this time public opinion was swinging against the arbitrary actions of the Government and after separate trials the three men were acquitted.

After Hardy's trial in October 1794 the crowd carried him and Thomas Erskine, who defended him, home in triumph. Burns was so enthused that he committed one of his most famous indiscretions. On 12th January 1795 he wrote to Mrs. Dunlop:

> 'Thank God, these London trials have given us a little more breath and I imagine that the time is not far distant when a man may freely blame Billy Pitt (the Prime Minister) without being called an enemy of his country.'

Commenting in the same letter on the executions of the French King and Queen in the previous year he asked:

> 'What is there in the delivering over of a perjured Blockhead and an unprincipled prostitute to the hands of the hangman, that it should arrest for a moment attention in an eventful hour, when, as my friend Roscoe in Liverpool gloriously expresses it—
>
> 'When the welfare of millions is hung in the scale,
> And the balance yet trembles with fate.'

Mrs. Dunlop was deeply offended and appears to have broken off relations with Burns until the last few days of his life. In the same period he was busy with the poem 'A Man's a Man for a' That.' Here is the purest expression of his democracy. In January 1795 Burns sends a copy of this poem to Thomson, with the following remarks:

> 'A great critic, Aitken, on songs, says that love and wine are the exclusive themes for song writing. The following is on neither subject and consequently no song; but will be allowed I think to be one or two pretty good prose thoughts inverted into rhyme'

He impressed on Thomson that the song was not for publication.

> 'I do not give you the foregoing song for your book (Thomson's *Select Scottish Airs*), but merely by way of vive la bagatelle; for the piece is not really poetry.'

Professor John Macunn, in his *Ethics of Citizenship*, has drawn attention to the close resemblance between Burns 'pretty good prose thoughts inverted into rhyme' and the attack on aristocracy in *The Rights of Man* the banned work of the other great exciseman, Thomas Paine.

A comparison between Paine's prose and Burns' poetryleaves no doubt of the correctness of this. Paine says:

> 'The patriots of France have discovered in good time that rank and dignity must take a new ground. It must now be the substantial ground of character, instead of titles.
>
> The artificial noble shrinks into a dwarf before the noble of nature.
>
> Through all the vocabulary of Adam there is not such an animal as a Duke or a Count.'

This pretty good prose thought is inverted into rhyme as:

A prince can mak' a belted knight,
A marquis, duke and a' that;

But an honest man's aboon his might,
Guid faith he mauna fa' that!
For a' that, and a' that,
Their dignities and a' that,
The pith o' sense and pride o' worth,
Are higher rank than a' that.

Paine ridicules aristocracy in memorable prose.

> 'The French constitution says there shall be no titles; and in consequence all that class of equivocal generation, which in some countries is called aristocracy and in others nobility is done away with and the peer is exalted into the man.
>
> Aristocracy talks about its fine blue ribbon like a girl and shows its new garter like a child.
>
> The genuine mind of man, thirsting for its native home, Society, condemns the gew-gaws that separate him from it.'

Burns expresses an identical thought with:

You see yon birkie ca'd a lord,
Wha struts, and stares, and a' that,
Though thousands worship at his word,
He's but a cuif for a' that.
For a' that, and a' that,
His ribband, star and a' that,
The man of independent mind
He looks and laughs at a' that.

'For what we can foresee all Europe may be one great Republic and man will be free of the whole,' says Paine. The similar thought is expressed in the immortal:

Then let us pray that come it may,

(As come it will for a' that,)
That Sense and Worth o'er a' the earth
Shall bear the gree for a' that,
For a' that, an a' that,
It's comin' yet for a' that,
That man to man the world o'er,
Shall brithers be for a' that.

Burns could be intimidated, temporarily, through fear of the suffering which his family would endure if he were victimised, but he could not be silenced for long. In one way or another he had to give expression to his true feelings.

His relation to the great French Revolution is well expressed by Professor G. P. Gooch in his chapter on 'Europe and the French Revolution' in the *Cambridge Modern History*. After pointing out that no political book supporting the Revolution had been published in Scotland he says:

> 'In literature certain French ideas found an eminent representative. In the uprising of the common people Burns saw the reflection of his own passionate hatred of social inequality . . . The philosophical and abstract side of the Revolution left him untouched. It was the struggle for equality based on the conception of a common manhood that stirred his enthusiasm and drew music from his lyre.'

The Dumfries Volunteers

In 1794 there settled in Dumfries Dr. William Maxwell, who had received his medical education in France, had been an enthusiastic supporter of the Revolution and as a member of the National Guard was present at the execution of King Louis XVI. Together with Burns and John Syme, who held the office of Distributor of Stamps for Dumfriesshire, he was regarded as the centre of Dumfries radicalism.

A 'True Loyal Natives' club had been formed in Dumfries 'for preserving the Peace, Liberty and Prosperity; and for supporting the laws and constitution of the country.' Burns and his friends were naturally the target of their attacks. One of their anti-Burns squibs read:

> Ye sons of Sedition, give ear to my song,
> Let Syme, Burns and Maxwell pervade every throng,
> With Cracken, the attorney, and Mundell, the quack,
> Send Willie, the monger, to hell with a smack.

Burns lost no time in framing his crushing reply:

Ye true 'Loyal Natives' attend to my song;
In uproar and riot rejoice the night long,
From Envy and Hatred, your corps is exempt,
But where is your shield from the darts of Contempt.

As Burns was putting his finishing touches to 'A Man's a Man for a' That' an invasion scare was sweeping the country. The Jacobins—the left small middle-class democrats had split and had been overthrown in France, but the more right wing groups, representing the main body of emerging French capitalism which had replaced them, were in no conciliatory mood with regard to Great Britain. Threats to invade Britain were a prominent feature of their speeches and this enabled the British Government to launch a great invasion scare and to call upon all loyal citizens to rally to the defence of their country. Companies of volunteers were formed everywhere.

On 31st January 1795 a meeting was held in the Dumfries Court House, at which it was decided to form a volunteer company for the town. Burns' name, together with that of Syme and Maxwell were amongst the signatories asking the permission of the authorities for the company to be formed. When permission was granted Burns and Syme joined and played an active part in the organisation. Maxwell did not. Doubtless in the interval he had grasped the politics behind the scare. Some critics have suggested that Burns' action in joining was largely make-believe; that desiring promotion as an exciseman he sought to stand in well with the Government. This overlooks the fact that most middle class and petty middle class radicals throughout Scotland who neither expected nor desired favours of the Government, did likewise. They were susceptible to the wave of chauvinism that was sweeping the country. Their arguments were that an invasion of Britain by France would not promote political reform. Some of them even calculated that a mass rally to national defence would weaken the drive that the Government was making against political reformers of all shades—which events soon showed to be a sad misjudgement.

The volunteer records show that Burns was an assiduous member of the company until his health broke down a few weeks before his death.

On 5th May 1795 the patriotic ballad, 'Does Haughty Gaul Invasion Threat,' appeared in the *Dumfries Journal.* This is the one poem the Tory Burnsites seize upon to prove that Burns was not as radical as some people imagine.

There are two versions of how the ballad came to be written. One is that Burns at a volunteers' gathering proposed the toast:

> 'Gentlemen, may we never see the French and the French never see us.'

On a certain captain taking umbrage, Burns, it is said, wrote the ballad and sent it to the journal. This is so like the case of Captain Dods that one is inclined to think that tradition is presenting the same incident in a new context.

The other is that his fellow volunteers expected some kind of poetical tribute to the volunteers and Burns obliged, managing to combine his own sentiments with those of a more traditional kind.

> O, let us not, like snarling tykes,
> In wrangling be divided,
> Till, slap! come in an unco loun,
> And wi' a rung decide it!
> Be Britain still to Britain true,
> Amang oursels united;
> For never but by British hands
> Maun British wrangs be righted!

That there were British wrangs and that they ought to be righted was hardly the True Loyal Nature creed.

The wretch that would a tyrant own,
  And the wretch, his true-sworn brother,
Who would set the mob above the throne,
  May they be damn'd together!
Who will not sing God Save the King
  Shall hang as high's the steeple;
But while we sing God Save the King,
  We'll ne'er forget the People!

This is precisely what the reactionaries were doing, singing 'God Save the King' and oppressing the People. So the Dumfries Volunteers got their ballad and the poet's friends had reason to rejoice. There was a powerful shot of reform principles even there.

A Rebel until Death

How absurd it is to claim that Burns was becoming reconciled to mad old George III and his monstrous brood of princely profligates can be seen in one of the last political ballads he wrote. At the end of 1795 the Government introduced new sedition Bills extending the meaning of treason and giving the magistrates power to break up meetings without reading the Riot Act. Henry Erskine, Dean of the Faculty of the Advocates in Edinburgh, brother of the famous Thomas Erskine, came out energetically against the new Bills, thereby enraging the majority of the advocates who on 12th January 1796 elected Robert Dundas of Ormiston in his place by 128 votes to 38. Dundas is the 'Pious Bob' and Erskine 'Squire Hal' in Burns' ballad, 'The Dean of Faculty,' from which we take the following characteristic verses:

This Hal for genius, wit and lore,
    Among the first was numbered,
But pious Bob, 'mid Learning's store,
    Commandment the Tenth remembered,
Yet simple Bob the victory got,
    And wan his heart's desire,
Which shows that Heaven can boil the pot,
    Tho' the Deil piss in the fire.

Squire Hal, besides, had in this case,
    Pretensions rather brassy;
For talents to deserve a place,
    Are qualifications saucy.
So their worships of the Faculty,
    Quite sick of Merit's rudeness,
Chose one who should owe it all, d'ye see
    To their gratis grace and goodness.

In your heretic sins may you live and die,
    Ye heretic Eight-and-Thirty,
But accept, ye sublime Majority,
    My congratulations hearty,
With your honours, as with a certain king,
    In your servants this is striking.
The more incapacity they bring
    The more they're to your liking.

The hand of death was already upon him when he was writing this ballad and six months afterwards he was dead.

He worked to the last, writing and perfecting songs for 'Thomson's *Select Scottish Airs.*' Nor was his old friendly enemy forgotten.

Ah Nick! Ah Nick! It is na fair
First showing us the tempting ware,
Bright wines and bonnie lassies rare
                To put us daft.
Syne weave unseen, thy spider snare
        O' Hell's damned waft.

He passed from the world on 21st July 1796 at the early age of thirty-seven leaving behind a legacy of song and verses that Scotsmen will ever be proud of, and a record of struggle against hypocrisy and privilege that will inspire his fellow-countrymen to continue the fight until the system that gives rise to them is superseded by a new and better social order.

His fight for liberty, equality and fraternity is our fight—in a new setting! He will be remembered and honoured in our country, and in the world, long after class society has been relegated to the dustbin of history.

Burns takes his place, and a foremost one, in the procession of Great Scottish Rebels who have striven to make the lot of the common people a happier one. And now the common people themselves, with ever-growing unity and determination, go forward to achieve their freedom and to make our beloved country a land of which Burns would be proud.